24,84

# THE GAMES
# THE INDIANS PLAYED

# The Games the Indians Played

SIGMUND A. LAVINE

*Illustrated with photographs and old prints*

DODD, MEAD & COMPANY
NEW YORK

PICTURE CREDITS
Courtesy of The Museum of the American Indian, Heye Foundation, p. 43; National
Park Service, p. 42. All other photographs courtesy of the Smithsonian Institution
National Anthropological Archives.

*For Jane—*
*from whom I have drawn so much*

# CONTENTS

*Model of Zuñi altar honoring A'hayuta, one of the gods of war. Note the offerings—many are used in various games.*

# 1. INTRODUCTION

*"Variety is the mother of enjoyment."*

As drums pound furiously, the teams take their positions and hundreds of spectators send up a cheer that echoes across the playing field. When the umpire gives the signal to start the game, a sudden hush falls over the crowd. But as soon as play begins, silence gives way again to a thunderous roar.

The excited crowd described had not gathered to witness the start of a world series, see the tie-breaking match in a Stanley Cup play-off, or watch a Rose Bowl game. Actually, the scene is typical of what took place when large numbers of American Indians—a people who honored outstanding athletes as highly as they did brave warriors—assembled to watch a sporting event. But the redman was not just an enthusiastic spectator. Indian men, women, and children engaged in games of many kinds for the sheer joy of competition.

Certain of these pastimes tested the strength, skill, or stamina of the players. As a result, such games not only furnished recreation but also served to train the young men of many tribes in the skills needed by a warrior. This is why the Cherokee called games "the little brother of war."

Generally speaking, American Indian games fell into two

classifications. The first consisted of games of chance, the second in games of dexterity. These, in turn, were divided in two —chance roughly into stick and dice or guessing games; dexterity into games of ball or training.

In one type of games of chance, dice of various materials— reeds, sticks, stones, or other objects marked or colored to represent agreed upon values—were tossed by the players who kept track of gains or losses with kernels of corn, pebbles, sticks, or beans. Similar counters were used in guessing games, in which one or more individuals attempted to guess where an object had been hidden.

Although players could develop certain techniques in games of chance, success or failure was fundamentally a matter of luck. But fortune played little part in the second group of games, which required both physical agility and quick thinking. Besides the various ball games, games of dexterity included archery; throwing spears at a rolling, netted wheel; casting lances so that they glided over ice or snow; racing long distances, the contestants often kicking a stick before them as they ran; and horseback riding.

Because the same games, with slight variations in equipment and rules, were played by Indians throughout the Americas, it is believed that they originated with the redman and were not borrowed from the whites. Moreover, enthnologists—students of the origins and cultures of the various races—have discovered that myths in which legendary heroes or divinities play games with a foe of mankind and defeat him are common to most tribes.

Many of these tales tell of the Divine Twins, children of the sun. Some hold that the moon was their mother, sister, or wife. Still others refer to the moon as their Twins' grandmother, or trace a relationship between them and the Spider Woman who

10

*Zuñi shuttlecocks made from cornhusks and feathers. These were bounced off the hand.*

traditionally taught man to spin. Tribal lore claims that the Twins were equal in magical powers and constantly contended with one another by playing games of chance and dexterity, which they taught to man when the world was young.

Not only did the Indians consider the Divine Twins (or their counterparts) the patrons of play but also the redman derived the equipment he used in different sports from their weapons. These included throwing clubs, netted shields, and bows that shot not only the arrow of destiny but the arrow of "far-seeing" which was tipped with "the heart of fact." Besides their weapons, the Twins also carried magical devices—the shuttlecock of divination, the tubes of hidden things, and the sticks of swift journeys. These, too, were transformed into gaming implements.

According to the storytellers, both Twins bore identical weapons and owned the same wondrous articles. Therefore, in order to identify his possessions, each Twin inscribed them

11

with distinguishing symbols—the source of the marks that determine the value of objects used in games of chance.

Because of their supposed divine origin, games were played originally by the Indians only to bring rain, insure rich harvests, cure illness, expel evil spirits, or to give pleasure to the gods. During these ceremonial contests the opposing players were considered representatives of the Divine Twins. This was particularly true of the Indians of the Southwest who worshipped the Twins as the gods of war and placed articles used in various games on their altars as sacrifices.

As indicated, the mythology of the redman contains countless tales in which the spirits of good and evil wager their respective magical powers on the outcome of various games. Thus it was only natural that these accounts of betting by the legendary creators of games prompted the Indians to gamble. Writing in 1778, Jonathan Carver, who wandered throughout the Northwest in the mid-eighteenth century seeking an overland route to the Pacific, reported that the Indians risked "their apparel, all moveables of their cabins, and sometimes their liberties." Assiniboin women were such avid gamblers that they would even bet their children's clothing. No wonder their husbands forbade them to play certain games and, if they disobeyed, spanked them!

# 2. GAMES OF CHANCE – STICK AND DICE

*"And now let's see your game."*

## Stick Games

No games of chance were more popular with Indian women than stick games. These pastimes ranged from a form of jackstraws in which two opponents picked up sticks (decorated to show their values) with forked twigs to various guessing games. In fact, so many stick games were guessing games that it is difficult to classify them. In the simplest type of stick guessing game, one contestant divided a bundle of sticks behind his back and challenged his rival to guess which hand held a specially marked stick or an odd and even number of sticks.

Other stick games were played by groups. Players would pass a stick from hand-to-hand until the leader of the other side pointed to the individual he thought had it. A correct choice won the game. Equally popular was a game in which one side hid a stick under one of several mounds of bark, grass, or straw and dared the other side to find it. This was not as easy as it appears. Not only did the person concealing the stick move his hands very quickly but also he made faces and twisted his body in all directions in hope of distracting the opposition's attention.

*This picture of Paiutes playing a guessing game was taken near the Grand Canyon by a member of the Powell Expedition, 1871–1875. Note the tally sticks, used to keep score, in front of the gamblers.*

The most complicated version of the game of locating a hidden stick was played by Alaskan tribesmen. Unlike other Indians, they did not use one stick but fifty-seven. Varying numbers of these sticks—which bore symbolic carvings or represented animals—were hidden by the leader under piles of moss. To win, a player not only had to guess which mounds contained certain sticks but also accumulate the most points. Scores were determined by the agreed worth of each carving.

Whether two or twenty inches long, the sticks used in all these games were symbolic of the arrows carried by the Divine Twins. So were the reeds and straws employed by some tribes. No special wood was used to fashion gaming sticks. For example, the Cree—whose bundles always contained an uneven number—made their sticks from willow, while Sioux children formed the "counting stick stalks" with which they played "odd or even" from sumac twigs. The most unusual sticks were those of Piegan youngsters. They played stick games with the pencils given to them at reservation schools.

Consistent winners at stick games were highly regarded. But most successful gamblers modestly claimed that their good fortune was due to the aid of friendly spirits and never bragged of their good fortune except while picking up their winnings. However, William Wood, writing in 1635 of the "strange whimsies" of New England tribes, states that "he who is a noted gambler hath a great hole in his ear wherein he carries his puims (sticks) in defiance of his antagonists."

The greatest honor a clever stick-game player could receive was to be appointed the leader of a side in an intertribal contest. There is an excellent description of one of these competitions in the journal kept in 1744 by Father P. de Charlevois, a French missionary in what is present-day Michigan:

That day the Pottawatomi had come to play the game of straws

*Group of Chippewa playing stick game at the village of Sagawa'mick on the shore of Mille Lac, Minnesota, in 1900. The house in the rear is made of elm bark.*

with the Miami. They played in the hut of the chief, and in a place opposite. These straws are small, about as thick as a wheat straw and two inches long. Each player takes a bundle of them, usually containing two hundred and one, always an uneven number.

After having well shaken them about, making meaningful a thousand contortions and invoking the spirits, they separate them, with a sort of thorn or polished bone, into parcels of ten. Each one takes his own haphazard, and he who has chosen the parcel containing eleven wins a certain number of points, as may have been agreed upon. . . . They also told me that there is as much skill as chance in this game; . . . that they give themselves up to it and spend whole days and nights at it; that sometimes they do not stop playing until they are entirely naked, having no more to lose.

A few tribes played a game that required only four sticks rather than the bundles of ten or more sticks used by most

Indians. Two of the four were identically decorated or were considerably shorter than the other pair. All four sticks were placed under a blanket or other covering and players attempted to guess their relative positions. Giving the stick's correct order won both the game and the right to hide the sticks. But guessing incorrectly did not necessarily mean losing. If the sticks lay in certain combinations (which varied among different tribes) a wrong guess did not count and a player was given another chance.

Instead of sticks, the Indians of the Northwest Coast played a similar game with four discs, one painted black, the others white. The Twana claimed that the first set of these gaming discs were given to them by a god who soon regretted the gift because the Indians did nothing but play with them. Therefore, he gathered up the discs and cast them into the ocean, only to have the waves wash them upon the shore. The god then threw the discs as far as he could, but they came rolling back. Nor could he destroy them by fire. Admitting defeat, the god decreed that the Indians could continue their gaming.

Puget Sound tribes took full advantage of this legend, using it as an excuse to hold intertribal disc games in which fortunes were won and lost. During these contests, singers and drummers on both sides appealed to the spirits for aid and made as much noise as possible to encourage their teams and confuse their opponents. Frequently, these "cheering sections" became too tired to continue their task. There was good reason—a game lasted until one side or the other lost all it possessed.

California Indians were as keen players of the four-stick game as the disc-using tribes. When unsuccessful, they blamed their poor luck on the presence of evil spirits and, to drive these demons away, cut gashes in their legs from the knee to the ankle. However, no matter how great their loss at stick games, the Indians rarely expressed resentment or jealousy, or disputed

*Group of California Indians playing a version of the stick game. Copy of a lithograph after a drawing by Louis Choris, made in the vicinity of San Francisco Bay, about 1818.*

the scoring. Such outbursts were considered displeasing to the gods of play. Losers left a game silently, secretly vowing to play again as soon as they had accumulated a stake to bet.

The hold the four-stick game had on the Indians and their compulsion to gamble while playing it are well illustrated by a tale told by the Takulli of British Columbia. It deals with a young man who was very fond of *atlih* (stick game) and was such a reckless gambler that he not only lost all his belongings but also his wife and children. Disgusted at his actions, his fellow tribesmen drove him from the village and the unlucky gambler wandered through the forest, cold and hungry. Suddenly, he came upon a great lodge and when he peeked through a chink in its wall he saw an old man seated before a roaring fire. Before the gambler could back away, the old man called, "Come in, my son-in-law. What are you doing out in the snow?"

Once inside, the young man told his story. The old man said nothing but summoned his daughter and commanded her to bring their guest food and richly beaded clothing. After eating and dressing, the gambler was given a sleeping robe and was warned by the old man not to leave the lodge under any circumstances.

Actually, the young man had no desire to leave. The lodge was warm, food was plentiful and well cooked, and the old man's daughter was beautiful. But as winter gave way to spring, the gambler became bored and, to pass the time, made a set of gaming sticks. When the old man saw them he said, "You will never be happy until you win at *atlih*. So be it. Take a bundle of furs, find your people, and play with them. My magic will make you win. But once you have won all that you can carry, throw your sticks away and come back at once."

The next morning the young man set out to find his kinsmen and, eventually, located their camp. They accepted his challenge to play *atlih* and, as the old man predicted, lost every game. Finally, realizing that he could not carry any more winnings back to the lodge, the gambler left the other players and went to the edge of the clearing. But, just as he was about to throw his sticks into the woods, he felt a powerful urge to play *atlih* one more time. Returning to the game, he lost not only his winnings and the old man's furs but also his clothing. Fearful of the reception he would receive at the lodge, the gambler retraced his steps. But search as he would, he never found the old man's dwelling again.

*Dice Games*

Centuries ago—according to tradition—the Navajo left their original home beneath the Earth and migrated upward into the present-day world. But the ground was too wet for them to establish their villages. While waiting for it to dry, the women played *tsindi*, a dice game they had learned in the netherworld.

This legend is partially supported by fact. A great many sets of dice have been unearthed in prehistoric ruins throughout the Southwest and in Colorado and Utah by archaeologists. These students of ancient cultures estimate that the Indians have been playing with dice for at least two thousand years. Research has also revealed that nearly every Indian tribe enjoyed gaming with dice.

However, the dice of the redmen have little in common with those employed to play backgammon, pachisi, Monopoly, and other games. Such dice are cubical in shape, each of their six faces bearing from one to six dots representing a number. The dice cast by the Indians were two-sided. One side was usually blank while the other was carved, painted, or decorated with lines that formed geometric patterns. These markings varied from tribe to tribe. So did the rules for tallying the relative worth of the designs, scoring being determined by the number of marked sides or combinations of designs which showed after a toss.

While cubical dice are generally made of bone, ivory, or plastic, the Indians fashioned theirs from a wide range of materials. Oregon tribes made dice from beaver and woodchuck teeth; Plains Indians used the anklebones or ribs of bison (buffalo); the Passamaquoddy, mussel shells; the Osage, pumpkin seeds. Dice were also manufactured from bark, corn kernels, fruit pits, horn, nut shells, pottery discs, and wooden chips. But the most common materials were thin pieces of wood, bone, cane, or reeds. These were split through the middle so that each half was round on one side, flat on the other. Thus, even if they were not decorated, score could be kept by counting how many round or flat sides were face upward.

Wins and losses at dice and other games of chance were recorded by counters exchanged by the players. These "chips" had many forms—beans, corn kernels, feathers, sticks, and stones. One anthropologist reports that during a game played by the Sioux in 1873, the tally was kept with umbrella ribs! Incidentally, some Indians blew on their counters before wagering them, just as modern gamblers "blow on the bones" for luck.

Sets of stick dice consisted of between three and fifteen pieces, the most common number being four. Usually long and narrow and between three and four inches long, they were cast by hand onto the ground. In most tribes only the men played stick dice. However, the favorite pastime of Havasupai women was gaming with three stick dice which were painted red on one side, white on the other. If three white sides showed after a throw, a player won ten counters; two whites and a red, two counters; two reds and a white, three counters; all reds, five counters.

*This picture of White Mountain Apache women playing stick dice was taken long before cameras were perfected. Nevertheless, despite lack of clearness, the dice can be seen in mid-air.*

During the New Year's feast of the Onondaga, the men competed against the women in a stick-dice game. If the latter won, it was considered a sign that the tribe would harvest only short ears of corn. But a victory by the men was held to augur an abundance of long ears. Actually, allowing women to play in a ceremonial stick-dice game held to divine the future, cure the sick, bring rain, or to honor the gods was very unusual. In most tribes, women were not even permitted to touch stick dice.

Gaming with stick dice during healing rituals and at religious rites stemmed from the many traditions in which either gods or legendary heroes tossed dice with masters of black magic and won. The Passamaquoddy tell of a contest in which Old Age was defeated by the Spirit of Youth whose friend, K'cheballock, the wind, controlled the fall of the dice. Nohoilpi, the gambling god of the Navajo, was also defeated by trickery when he played Hatsehogan, a culture hero. Hovering above the game which was played at dusk, a bat caught Hatsehogan's sticks and dropped them so that they registered the best possible count. Certain New Mexico tribesmen claim that stick dice were invented by Gau-pot, greatest of gamblers, who staked his eyes in a game with the sun and lost.

Because many tribes believed that the incantations chanted to bring good fortune at stick dice drove away evil spirits, sick individuals often asked their friends to play a game so that they would recover. Before the contest, several practice games were held and all who played in them fasted and prayed in hopes of dreaming that they would win the ritual competition. Such dreams were believed positive proof that the game would achieve its purpose. Thus the dreamer was automatically chosen to represent the ailing member of the tribe at the ritual game.

It was a great honor to represent either the sick individual or the demon that was supposedly causing his illness. But the

Wahpeton band of Sioux thought it an even greater glory to be picked to impersonate a ghost at a most unusual stick-dice game. These unique contests were held when a wealthy man died to avoid any disputes over the sharing of his estate. The deceased's ghost—a respected member of the community—divided the dead man's property into lots of equal value and then played stick dice with each heir in turn. The heirs wagered nothing and competed with the ghost until they won. Then their place was taken by another.

*Sholiwe*, the stick-dice game of the Zuñi, was originally played by priests to divine the outcome of a battle. The sticks they used were decorated to represent the four quarters of the Earth, the seasons, fire, air, moisture, and the masculine and feminine elements in nature. Made of split cane, the sticks fitted into one another and their pairing was an important factor in the game.

A game of *sholiwe* was also played at the Zuñi festival honoring the gods of war, who were considered patrons of stick dice. One of the many games the gods had traditionally played was with Mi-si-na, the eagle star god whose head can be seen in the Milky Way. Because Mi-si-na lost, eagles became the war god's servants—which is why eagle feathers are used to fletch war arrows.

Legend also holds that the war gods tossed stick dice to make it rain. Therefore, the pueblo dwellers organized a fraternity to compete at *sholiwe* in times of drought. Ceremonial games in which representatives of the various clans took part were also held to forecast the future. Whenever *sholiwe* was played for ritual purposes, the stakes were white shell beads. These beads are practically identical with the wampum of Atlantic coast tribes.

No stick-dice game was more popular in the Southwest than

*Skill was as important as luck when playing* pa-tol. *The "rivers" and "horses" can be seen in this early painting of a game.*

*pa-tol,* which was played with three sticks incised with patterns of diagonal lines. Before a contest, the players made a four-foot circle with forty fist-sized stones and placed a flat rock about six inches square in its center. Openings were left between every tenth and eleventh stone. Called "rivers," these gaps were located at the cardinal compass points.

The players—usually there were four—sat around the circle at the rivers. Each, in turn, threw the dice by lifting them chin high, then suddenly casting them as if to harpoon the flat rock in the center of the circle. All the sticks landed on their ends and rebounded inside the stone enclosure.

According to his score, a player moved his "horse" (a twig or stone) in a clockwise or counter-clockwise direction from a river. The winner was the player who completed the circuit first. However, if an opponent's horse landed on a stone that was already occupied, the first player had to start over again. As a result, skilled *pa-tol* players attempted to lag behind until they were in a position to win. This not only lessened the chances of their own horse being "killed" but also gave more opportunities to land on their rivals' markers. Actually, it took as much skill as luck to win at *pa-tol*. An expert could almost always make the dice fall with the markings he wanted showing. This was done by the manner in which the sticks were arranged in the hand and the force with which they were thrown.

### Basket-dice Games

Besides casting stick dice by hand, the Indians also tossed dice in a basket or wooden bowl. Some tribes shook the container, then threw the dice against a target or onto the ground. Others tossed the dice upward, then caught them. Still others struck the side of the basket to make the dice tumble about.

*Painting (about 1895) by Mary Irvin Wright shows Menominee men playing the bowl game.*

Just as stick dice were symbolic of the Divine Twins' arrows, the baskets and bowls used in dice games were emblematic of their shields. Moreover, southwestern tribes frequently wove representations of such legendary figures as Eagle Man, the crony of gamblers, at the bottom of baskets employed for gaming. The container used by the Micmac was derived from the wooden bowl they filled with water and left standing overnight so the shamans could foretell the future according to the amount of evaporation that had taken place. The bowl, itself, stemmed from the shell of Mikchitch, the turtle, who was the companion of Glooscap, a Micmac demigod. Traditionally, Mikchitch established the value of the counters used in dice games.

*Decorated pottery bowl showing Eagle Man, the crony of gamblers, and marked with representations of gaming reeds. Hopi.*

26

In general, basket-dice games were simple, although some took considerable skill. The easiest to play were those in which the dice were freely cast and scores determined by their markings. Games in which the container was hit in order to make a specially marked bean, seed, stone, tooth, or other object jump out or fall with a decorated side uppermost were far more difficult. Perhaps the most complicated dice games were played by the Eskimos and the Chippewa, who tossed a number of small carved figures of animals and birds onto the ground in an attempt to have them either stand upright or face their opponents.

Basket-dice games were played mostly by women. The Ponca say this is because the first basket dice were made by Ukiaba, a tribal hero who gave the original set—five plum stones—to a beautiful maiden in order to win her love. The tradition that the maiden never lost when playing with Ukiaba's gift is probably the reason why so many tribes made dice from plum stones.

After cleaning and drying plum stones, Omaha women burned them until they were black. The carbon was cut away on two of them so as to form a crescent moon on one side, a star on the other; while all the carbon was removed from one side of the remaining stones, allowing their natural color to show. The incised designs in combination with the burned or natural sides had the following values:

| | |
|---|---|
| 2 moons and 3 natural stones | 10 points |
| 2 stars and 3 black stones | 10 points |
| 1 moon, 1 star, and 3 natural stones | 1 point |
| 1 moon, 1 star, and 3 black stones | 1 point |

No other casts counted. Nor did a throw in which the stones spilled out of the basket. A player continued until she failed to toss a winning combination, taking counters (twigs or blades of grass) from her opponent until all were won.

Basket-dice games were noisy contests. Roger Williams, one of the few early colonists to treat the Indians fairly, records that when the Narragansett cast plum stones "burnt on one side, plain on the other," they did so "with a mighty noise of swearing . . . desiring to make the gods side with them." But the Narragansett were not content to rely on incantations to bring them good fortune. Like many present-day gamblers, they carried good-luck charms. None of these was considered more powerful than a stone dug up under a tree hit by lightning.

Incidentally, Williams was not the only one to remark about the noise made by players of basket dice. William Wood states that the Indians of Massachusetts shouted "Hub Hub" so loudly that they could be heard at a distance of a quarter of a mile. Their cries still echo in dictionaries, where the word "hubbub" is defined as "a loud noise of many voices shouting at once."

# 3. GAMES OF CHANCE – GUESSING

*"At the game's end we shall see who gains."*

Guessing games were common to all Indian tribes. Most of these pastimes, like the hidden-stick game previously mentioned, consisted of passing an object from hand-to-hand, or hiding it and defying others to find it. Another type of guessing game was similar to "Twenty Questions." For example, young Eskimo girls in Labrador would cup their hands around a small article while their playmates attempted to identify it by asking what it was made of, its color, and use.

Other guessing games were far more complicated. This is particularly true of certain of the redman's versions of "button, button, who has the button?" Among these was a game played by teams of Pima men. Before one of these contests began, the teams stood parallel, facing a goal, each player directly behind the man in front. At an agreed-upon signal, one team began passing a pottery disc back and forth. If the leader of the other side guessed who had the disc, he took possession of it. Meanwhile, his team's anchor man ran to the head of the line and jumped as far as he could toward the goal over the extended leg of the first man in line. If an incorrect guess was made, the disc did not change hands and the side that retained it did the jumping. The game ended when all the members of a team reached the goal.

Pima women never took part in these contests. Female participation in certain guessing games was also forbidden in other tribes. In still others, both sexes competed in guessing games, either separately or as a group. While Indians in warmer areas played guessing games throughout the year, those living in colder regions engaged in them only in the winter. The Kiowa were in the last-named category, as is shown by their word for a guessing game, *do-a*. This is a combination of *do* (house) and *a* (game).

Although the Indians deliberately tried to confuse their opponents when hiding or passing an object—some players hung buckskin thongs from their wrists and covered their fingers with scraps of fur—cheating was most unusual. In reporting on the few instances of cheating he observed during his years of studying Indian customs, Dr. Frank Russell states, ". . . there is reason to believe that this practice has arisen since they have come in contact with the whites."

There is little doubt that the redman checked any tendency to cheat because he believed that his gaming was watched by the gods. Nevertheless, tribal lore is crammed with details of how legendary figures bested their opponents by trickery while playing guessing games. Typical of these stories is the one told by the Maidu. These California Indians are famous for two things—their rich tribal culture and their habit of grunting while playing their favorite guessing game to attract the attention of their gods. The game consisted of picking which of two bundles of grass contained a marked cylinder. Maidu tradition holds that there was once an evil spirit who was very clever at guessing games. After winning everything owned by an opponent, the spirit would suggest one more game—the loser to stake his freedom against his former belongings. No one ever

*Too old to hunt or fight, these elders of the Paiute tribe pass their days gaming. This photograph was taken in Nevada in the 1870's.*

recouped and, as a result, the spirit had many slaves. Eventually, however, the slaves were set free by the son of the clouds, who won them from the spirit. But the young man's victory was not honestly gained—the sun told him in which bundle of grass the cylinder was hidden.

## Hidden Ball

Pshaiyanne, a Sia culture hero, is credited with besting an evil spirit in a game of hidden ball. This game was played only by the men, who usually competed in teams. The leader of one side would conceal a small object in one of four places, and the leader of the other side guessed where it was hidden. As in all Indian games, the method of scoring differed among the various tribes. In some instances, guessing correctly the first time only won the right to secrete the ball. Other Indians set definite values on their rival's three guesses. Thus, locating the ball on the first try won the largest number of counters; the third guess, the least. Irrespective of the method of scoring, the game continued until one side or the other had lost all its counters.

Afterward, the counters—which again might be sticks, stones, seeds, twigs, or pebbles—were redeemed for the articles wagered on the outcome of the game. Since umpires had carefully matched each man's bet against a bet of equal worth, the winners were content. Incidentally, the Crows did not need umpires to supervise their betting. Crow tally sticks were marked to show their value—so many horses, buffalo hides, or even a wife.

Actually, the name "hidden ball" is a misnomer. Besides balls made of fur, mesquite gum, stone, or wood, the Indians played with fruit pits, colored pebbles, beans, or small pieces of bone, horn, and wood.

There was as great a variation in the places the "balls" were concealed as in their character. Balls were hidden under strips

32

of hide, in narrow-mouthed containers, or specially fashioned holders. The Walapai hid their root balls in a shallow rut cut in sand. One player drew the ball along the bottom of the rut with one hand (dropping it at some point) while filling in the trench with the other hand. Then, he piled the sand into four more-or-less equal mounds and dared his competitors to guess which one contained the ball.

The Papago hid a bean in one of four reeds which were then filled with sand, while the Hopi used four sand-filled cottonwood cups. But most southwestern tribes concealed the ball in cane tubes.

All the tubes employed in hidden ball were decorated, but none bore more symbolic designs than those used by the Zuñi. This is because the Zuñi held the game sacred to the gods of war. Thus they engaged in ceremonial games of hidden ball in hopes of learning the outcome of a battle or causing it to rain, or to ask help from their divinities. Before playing in these ritual contests, the competitors fasted, prayed, and bathed. Similar rites are carried out today by the devout who place cane tubes used in hidden ball on the altars erected in pueblos during certain religious festivals.

Both the Navajo and the Apaches were avid players of hidden ball. But they engaged in the pastime only during the winter and at night. Despite traditions stating why the game was taboo at other times, these tribes had probably discovered that it was easier to conceal the ball in the dark than in sunshine. In fact, some players covered the slightest opening in their houses before a game in order to prevent their opponents' benefiting from the light of the moon. Others even blackened their faces so that it would be more difficult to note a change in their expressions when they hid the ball.

Jicarilla Apaches often sought the aid of their shamans before playing hidden ball and asked them for a magic strong enough to insure their winning. These Indians also sang and chanted—as did many other tribes—during a contest, believing that it would bring them good fortune.

Perhaps the most unusual of all hidden-ball games was one played by the Seneca. It took place after a funeral to bring comfort to the mourners. The songs sung at such competitions were slow and solemn. Moreover, if one of the players forgot himself and became excited during the game, he was severely admonished by the leader of his team who reminded the offender that this was no ordinary game. With the exception of a short intermission during which a ceremonial meal was eaten, play lasted from dusk to the break of dawn. Then, as the sun rose over the horizon, all the implements used by the players were destroyed.

*Moccasin Game*

If Navajo tradition is true, there was no light when the Earth was young except for the feeble illumination cast by eagle-plume torches. However, certain animals were convinced that they could find food easier if there were more light. On the other hand, some creatures wished to have the torches put out so that they could hunt in complete darkness.

The two groups constantly argued over the question of more or less light, and there seemed no way to resolve their dispute until the cunning coyote suggested that the matter be settled by a game of hidden ball. Because Yeitso, the "Great Destroyer" of Navajo legend, promised to help the night prowlers, they agreed. After holding a meeting—at which the gopher explained how he could thwart Yeitso—the animals that wanted more light decided to play. But the groups could not concur in the method of hiding the ball.

Eventually, both sides accepted the bear's suggestion that he bury his moccasins in sand and that they be used as the four

ABOVE: *"Guessing the location of the marked bullet." Chippewa playing the moccasin game at White Earth, Minnesota, about 1910.* BELOW: *Player with raised stick is about to point to where he thinks bullet is hidden.*

containers. This was done. But although the animals played for hours and large numbers of tally sticks were wagered on every guess, the game was a tie. Whenever the animals that wanted more light concealed the ball, Yeitso's magic located it. Meanwhile, the gopher would burrow under the moccasins each time the night prowlers hid the ball, feel them, and thus find the ball. At last, both sides decided that the game should be ended.

Because the contest was a tie, the animals agreed to compromise—from now on, there would be equal periods of light and darkness every day. As a result, the sun rose for the first time. Some of the animals were so frightened by the sight that they hid. Others sought the security of their dens. One of the latter was the wood rat who lived a considerable distance away. He ran home so fast that he raised calluses on his toes—and his descendants still bear them.

In his rush to get out of the blinding sunshine, the bear also suffered a misfortune. He was in such a hurry that he put his moccasins on the wrong feet. This is why, say the Navajo, a bear has misshapen paws.

No Navajo storyteller would recount the legend of the first moccasin game except on a winter's night. Nor did any member of the tribe dare to engage in the game or sing the songs associated with it at any other time. They believed that, if they did, a huge rattlesnake would mysteriously appear and bite them.

However, most Indians played the moccasin game throughout the year. Actually, it was the favorite gambling game of both men and women of many tribes. While the majority of players used four moccasins, certain Indians employed only two, others as many as eight.

Generally speaking, guessing which moccasin held the hidden object—this was usually indicated by pointing with a stick—on the first attempt won the greatest number of tally sticks. But as in all other Indian guessing games, the rules and methods of scoring differed from tribe to tribe. Moreover, there were many variations of the basic game.

One of the most unusual of these penalized a player if his first guess was correct. In this game four objects, one of which was specially marked, were hidden. Locating the marked object on the first and second tries resulted in a loss of four and three points respectively. Four points were awarded for a right guess on the third attempt and, if all three guesses were wrong, a player lost four points.

Singing to the accompaniment of drums in hopes of attracting the attention of the gods and confusing opponents was an important part of the moccasin game. When playing *ing-kee-ko-kee* (moccasin game), the Iowa chanted:

> Take care of yourself—shoot well, or you lose
> You warned me, but see, I have defeated you!
> I am one of the Great Spirit's Children.
> Wa-konda I am! I am Wa-konda!

While ceremonial moccasin games were played in honor of the gods or to ask favors of them, far more contests were held for the purpose of gambling. Indeed, no other guessing game was more used for gaming. Huge wagers were bet in some contests. Yet the stakes were not always high. One group of Chippewa played continually for a day and a half for two second-hand neckties!

Certain individuals became so fascinated by the game that they risked all their belongings on one guess. The Missisauga of Canada referred to a man who lost everything as *nah-bah-wan-yah-ze-yaid*. This can be freely translated as "one who has a piece of cloth with a string around his waist."

Early observers of Indian life filled their journals with notes detailing the redman's fondness for the moccasin game. Their reactions were varied. Some of them were amused by the Indi-

*Painting (about 1895) by Mary Irvin Wright of Menominee Indians play-
ing "at bullet." Note the sticks representing wagers in center of blanket.*

ans' compulsion to gamble. Others, who took the time to learn
tribal legends and traditions, painstakingly traced the religious
significance of the game. The idea that the game had any holy
associations shocked the devout missionaries who labored to
convert the Indians to Christianity. But the redmen continued
to play the moccasin game as they had for centuries. However,
the white man did influence the game. His bullets replaced the
traditional objects hidden in the moccasins.

When the United States Government rounded up the Indians and forcibly settled them on reservations, officials hoped
that many of the ancient customs would be cast aside. Many of
them were—but the moccasin game was more popular than
ever. Actually, the Indians had little else to do—soldiers kept
them from raiding their neighbors' horse herds, holding certain

age-old ceremonies, or even wandering freely about. The moccasin game filled what seemed, to the first generation of reservation Indians, endless days.

At first, the authorities paid little attention to the Indians' gambling. Then, as reports came in of men betting the rations and clothing given to them for their families, investigations were undertaken. As a result, the Sioux confined to the Pine Ridge Reservation in South Dakota were forbidden to play the moccasin game.

Strangely enough, white men had been barred from engaging in the moccasin game some years before this. The settlers in the Indiana Territory spent so much time playing a version of the game in which they hid a bullet that they neglected their crops. Therefore, a decree was issued making it a criminal offense for any man who was not an Indian to "play at bullet."

# 4. GAMES OF DEXTERITY—
## WITH BALLS

*"I do not in the least object to a sport*
*because it is rough."*

Among the curiosities carried back to Spain by Columbus after his second voyage to the New World was a ball. It had little resemblance to the balls then used by Europeans to play tennis, ninepins, and other games. These balls were made from inflated bladders or hair encased in leather. Not only did the solid and heavy ball displayed by the Great Admiral bounce far more freely than air- or hair-filled balls but also it was made of a material hitherto unknown in the Old World.

Columbus' ball was, of course, fashioned from rubber. Anxious to learn as much as they could about this strange substance, both Spanish savants and sportsmen sought information in the writings of the chroniclers who accompanied gold-seeking expeditions to Central America.

Rubber, they learned from one authority, ". . . is a resin of a special tree which when boiled becomes like sinews. . . . It has one property which is that it jumps and rebounds upward, and continues jumping from here to there so that those who run after it become tired before they catch it."

40

The noted Spanish historian Torquemada, writing in 1613, was more specific. "They make the ball," he states, "from the sap of a tree which grows in the hot country, from which trickle some white thick drops when it is punctured, and which very soon jell, which when mixed and kneaded, turns out blacker than pitch."

However, long before Torquemada described rubber, early explorers had set down detailed accounts of the ball games of the New World. Cortez, conqueror of Mexico, actually demonstrated how the Indians played with rubber balls at the court of Charles V of Spain. The game played by Cortez in 1528 was a combination of basketball, soccer, volleyball, and jai-alia (a fusion of tennis and handball in which balls are thrown and caught in a basket fastened to a glove worn by the players).

No one knows when a Central American tribesman first molded rubber into a ball and played with it. However, it must have been at a very early date. Figurines depicting ballplayers —estimated by archaeologists to be at least three thousand years old—have been unearthed at Tlatilco, Mexico. While these sculptures indicate that some sport involving a ball was enjoyed by the residents of the Valley of Mexico as early as 1500 B.C., they offer no hint as to how the game was played.

On the other hand, the formal ball court approximately two thousand years old which was discovered in the jungle surrounding the ancient community of Copan, Honduras, is exactly like the courts described in ancient manuscripts. Therefore, experts are convinced that other long-vanished courts were built long before Copan was settled. Archaeological research has also revealed that practically every pre-Columbian Indian community from El Salvador to central Arizona had at least one *tlachtli* (ball court).

Central American courts were paved, shaped like a capital **I**, and surrounded by high stone walls. Their length varied from 100 to 125 feet, their width from 20 to 50 feet. Usually, a stone hoop from six to eight inches in diameter was inserted vertically at the center of each of the two long walls. The players— teams consisted of as few as two or as many as a dozen men— attempted to shoot the ball through these hoops.

Contestants played the ball off the walls with such skill that, if they were well matched, it flew from one end of the court to the other for over an hour without touching the ground. If one side dropped the ball into the opponents' territory (one of the bases of the **I**), it scored. Points were also given to a team if its rival tried but failed to put the ball through the hoop. When a player succeeded in "shooting a basket," all previous scores were canceled and the game ended.

It was far from easy to get the five-pound solid rubber ball through the hoop. Rules forbade any player from touching the ball with feet, legs, or bare hands. The ball was kept in play by either batting it with a flat stone or by hitting it with the elbows, knees, or hips. To prevent injuries, the contestants wore knee and elbow pads made of quilted cotton and fastened belts or yokes around their waists. These were fashioned from leather or basketry. In some areas, yokes were made of stone and weighed as much as fifty pounds. While stone yokes undoubtedly gave the ball a better bounce, historians are agreed that, in general, stone yokes were only worn at pre-game ceremonies.

But despite belts, pads, and other protective devices, few players emerged from a game without a serious injury. One eyewitness reported: "Some of them were carried dead out of the place and the reason was that as they ran, tired, and out of breath, after the ball from one end to the other, they would see the ball come in the air and in order to reach it first before the others would rebound on the pit of their stomach or in the

42

hollow, so that they fell to the ground out of breath, and some of them died instantly, because of their ambition to reach the ball before anybody else. . . . They were so quick to hit their knees or seats that they returned the ball with extraordinary velocity. With these thrusts they suffered great damage on the knees or on the thighs, with the results that those who for smartness often used them, got their haunches so mangled that they had those places cut with a small knife and extracted blood which the blows of the ball had gathered."

Members of the winning team quickly forgot their bruises and broken bones because the spectators ladened them with

*Pottery figurine of a ball player wearing a yoke, holding hands in front of his chest, perhaps catching a ball or calling for it. State of Colima, Mexico.*

43

*Stone masonry ball court and amphitheater in the ruins at Wupatki National Monument, Arizona. These people were ancestors of the Hopi.*

valuable gifts. But the captain of the losing side didn't even have a chance to say, "Wait till next time." He was hauled off to the temple and ceremonially executed by the priests!

Just as North American Indians believed that their games originated with the gods, Central Americans were positive that their deities had been the first to use a ball in sport. They also held that their divinities played ball to settle disputes. Indeed, the accounts of the legendary contests of Quetzalcoatl, ruler of the air, and his twin brother Xolotl, companion of the sun, closely resemble the tales told of the Divine Twins.

Traditionally, Quetzalcoatl was a skilled ball-player. Therefore, many ball courts were dedicated to him. Other gods were also associated with the game. Low reliefs on the walls of courts still standing near Veracruz and Yucatan in Mexico not only depict players being sacrificed but also sacred figures. Incidentally, in pre-conquest Mexico, Xolotl was considered the patron of games of ball.

The religious background of the favorite sport of Central Americans led to decrees that no court be used until it had been blessed and dedicated by the priests "on a day of good omen with certain ceremony and witchcraft." But the religious rituals connected with the game did not stop people from gambling, whether amateurs or professionals were competing. The poor even sold their children in order to raise money to bet! Nobles and men of wealth wagered fortunes—chests of jewels, sacksful of cocoa, and vast areas of land. On one occasion, Axayacatlt, king of what is now Mexico City, ventured his yearly income against that of his neighbor Xihuitlemoc, ruler of Xochimilco.

In order to insure winning, gamblers prayed to the gods. At dusk they would place a ball and a player's equipment on a plate set atop a pole. Then, bowing or kneeling, they spoke to the gods "with certain words of superstition and incantations."

The **I**-shaped court was not the only type constructed. Some, like those excavated in Arizona, were sunk below the surface of the surrounding ground. In some instances, the vertical walls of the **I** floor plan were replaced by sloping side walls. Hoops, or the remains of them, are lacking in several existing courts. It is believed that there once was some form of goal painted at intervals along their length, a supposition strengthened by the presence of three intricately carved stone markers inserted in the floor of certain courts which probably were used in scoring. But no one knows. The peoples who used these courts left no records.

Meanwhile, although the Spanish conquerors in their zeal to convert the Indians destroyed every ball court they found, because "each was like a temple . . . with . . . two images of the god of the ball game," the rubber ball bounced into wider use. It not only changed the ancient game of tennis but also led to the development of volleyball. Then, too, it is very likely that the discovery of a Maya court at Chichan Itza in Yucatan motivated Dr. James E. Naismith to create a new game in 1892. It was played by five men on a side who attempted to throw the ball into their opponents' hoop. Although Naismith placed the hoops horizontally and the players were required to keep the ball in play with their hands, there is little doubt that both Quetzalcoatl and Xolotl would approve of basketball.

## Lacrosse

Once upon a time and long ago, according to Cherokee legend, a ball game was held between the animals and the birds. While the latter were preening their feathers before the contest, two small creatures scrambled up the tree in which the birds were roosting. The eagle, chief of the birds, seeing that the newcomers were four-footed, screamed, "Get out of here! You belong with the animals."

"They wouldn't let us play," replied one of the intruders. "They told us to go away because we are so small."

"Well," admitted the eagle, "small or not, we could use more players. But you're no use to us. You can't fly."

Just then the owl hooted to attract the eagle's attention, flew to him, and whispered in his ear. Then the owl ordered the hawk to zoom to where the insects sat drumming, rip a piece of hide off one of the drumheads, and bring it back as quickly as possible. This was done. Under the owl's direction, the birds fastened the bit of hide under the legs of one of the intruders. Meanwhile, the owl, using his powerful beak, pulled out the other creature's skin until it had stretched to his toes.

"Now we shall see," the owl grunted, and he threw a ball

46

*Menominee Indians playing lacrosse. Note the extremely small baskets on their rackets.*

into the air. As the ball was about to hit the ground, the hide-winged volunteer swooped under it, batted it upward with his nose, and his friend caught the ball in his teeth. The birds showed their approval by shrieking, whistling, cackling, and chirping.

Later they had good reason to applaud. During the game, the newcomers proved so clever at handling the ball—one keeping it aloft, the other carrying it in his mouth from treetop to treetop—that the birds won easily. Moreover, from that time to this, both Tlameha the bat and Tewa the flying squirrel have been winged.

Tlameha's and Tewa's legendary skill at keeping the ball in the air was envied by many Indians. These individuals engaged in various versions of a game in which a ball made of wood or buckskin stuffed with hair was thrown or scooped into a goal by sticks having a net at one end. Some tribes played with one

47

racket, others with two. But in either case, the ball was kept in play by the use of a racket. Touching it with the hands was forbidden.

While certain authorities believe that the bark strips employed by the Seneca to curve the bats originally used in the game led to the development of netted sticks, others disagree. They hold that the nets are derived from the spider-web shields of the Divine Twins. Irrespective of its origin, the netted stick is the source of the name the French settlers of Canada gave to the game in which it is used. Because the netted stick roughly resembles a crosier—the staff carried by a bishop of the Catholic Church—they called the game *la crosse*. Today, lacrosse is the national game of Canada as well as a popular sport elsewhere.

Although injuries are commonplace wherever modern lacrosse is played, the game is not nearly as dangerous as the Indian version. Few of the participants escaped severe bruises, while many suffered deep scalp wounds or broken bones. Indeed, engaging in lacrosse was so perilous that the Iroquois Confederation adopted "this extremely brutal pastime" as training for war. Nevertheless, while primarily a man's game, lacrosse was played by the women of certain tribes, but rarely on the same fields as the men. Among the Passamaquoddy, it was taboo for a man even to look at women playing lacrosse. The mythmakers claim that one man did and the furious women chased him into a lake where he was transformed into a fish.

To a Cherokee brave the idea of a female playing lacrosse was ridiculous. In his tribe, a racket was considered unfit for use if a woman touched it. At one time, the Cherokee put to death any female who came in contact with a racket, even if accidentally. On the other hand, both sexes of the Santee Sioux competed in lacrosse. The Shawnee not only permitted their

*Women playing ball on the prairie. Reproduced from an oil painted by Seth Eastman in the 1840's.*

women to play but also allowed them to break the fundamental rule of the game and touch the ball with their hands.

Actually, rules and techniques varied little from tribe to tribe. But there were differences in both the type of goal and the size of playing fields. Usually, the latter were quite long, ranging from five hundred feet to a mile or more in length. Indians living in settlements laid out permanent fields. Nomadic tribes had favorite sites on which they played as they wandered. The place where the Winnebago held their most important games is now Prairie de la Cross, Wisconsin.

A single post at either end of the field served some tribes as a goal. If the ball hit the post, it counted as a score. Other tribes used two posts—the Choctaw connected them with a crossbar—and the ball had to be put through them. The most unusual goal was that of the Muskogee. It consisted of a square mat that had to be hit.

49

George Catlin, who traveled throughout the West painting Indians and recording their activities in the early 1800's, claimed that lacrosse as played by the redman "can never be appreciated by those not happy to see it." Then he wrote:

It is no uncommon occurrence for six or eight hundred or a thousand of these young men, to engage in a game of ball, with five or six times that number of spectators. . . . Such a scene, with its hundreds of Nature's most beautiful models . . . running and leaping into the air . . . in desperate struggles for the ball . . . (is) equal to any of those which ever inspired the hand of the artist in the Olympian games or the Roman forum.

Lacrosse so delighted Catlin that he would ride thirty miles to see a game. He confessed:

I have almost dropped from the horse's back, with irresistible laughter at the succession of droll tricks, and kicks and scuffles which ensue in the almost superhuman struggle for the ball. These plays generally commence at nine o'clock, or near it, in the morning; and I have more than once balanced myself on my pony, from that time to near sundown, without more than one minute of intermission at a time, before the game has been decided.

The "droll tricks" of lacrosse players may have amused Catlin but they kept the umpires busy stopping fights—their only other duty was to throw the ball into the air when it landed on the ground. While fights often caused injuries, they never led to hard feelings after a game. Such an attitude would be unpleasing to the gods. For the same reason, cheating was extremely rare, as indicated.

However, the storytellers insist that if a player hadn't cheated in a game held long ago, there would be no moon, which came into being when the player cast the ball toward the goal with his hand. Instead of flying straight, the ball arched upward and became fixed in the sky. Thus the moon serves to remind all who play lacrosse that they should not cheat. Moreover, if the moon is small and pale, it is a sign that someone has handled the ball unfairly.

Because of this legend, certain tribes would only play lacrosse when the moon was full. But no matter when a game was held, both participants and spectators bet heavily on its outcome. Yet lacrosse, like most Indian games, was allied with the redman's religious beliefs. As a result, the Huron played the game not only for recreation but also to cure sickness. Before every contest the players offered prayers asking the gods for help. They also sought the aid of charms, tucking the wings of a swift-flying bird into their breechclouts or hanging the tail of an antelope or deer from their wrists to give them speed.

Of all pre-game ceremonies, those engaged in by the Cherokee before a contest between two towns were the most complicated. For three weeks before the event, the players could not eat sluggish fish, vegetation with brittle stalks, salt, or hot foods. They were also forbidden to eat the flesh of the rabbit because it is a timid animal, or to touch an infant because its bones are easily broken.

The night before the game, both sides held an all night dance during which their opponents were defied with chants, shouts, and gestures. Meanwhile, the players secretly met with a shaman at a nearby body of water and underwent a ritual cleansing. At sunrise they set out for the field, making four stops on the way during which each man was given individual guidance. After receiving it, along with a talisman, a player was not allowed to lean against anything but the back of one of his teammates while sitting on the ground.

At the final stop, the shaman gave the players a "peptalk," just as a football coach does today before a contest. Like his modern counterpart, the shaman also held "skull drill" by drawing a game plan in the sand. Then, with the aid of the

*Cherokee pre-ballgame dance at Qualla Reservation, North Carolina, 1888.* ABOVE: *Dance has just begun—ball sticks are hanging on rack. Seven women dancers stand in a row behind woman's dance leader, who is seated with drum.* BELOW: *The ballplayers hold ball sticks up while moving counter-clockwise around the fire. Their leader—at extreme right of picture—shakes a gourd rattle.*

*"Ball Play on the Prairie"—engraving after a painting by Seth Eastman, 1852. The players are Sioux.*

shaman and his assistants, the players made twenty-eight scratches on each arm and leg and cut an **X** on their chests with a sacred comb made from a turkey bone.

Finally, appealing to the water for strength, to Red Bat for skill in dodging, to Red Deer for speed, to Red Hawk for keen sight, and to Red Rattlesnake to fill their opponents' hearts with fear, the players ran onto the field.

While the shouts of hundreds of players in intertribal lacrosse games are no longer heard on the prairie, equally exciting contests are engaged in by the North American Lacrosse Association, a league of eight teams that play "box lacrosse" in iceless hockey rinks. According to one sportswriter, this game draws its rules from ice hockey, field lacrosse, and "what used to be called 'murder ball' on grammar school playgrounds (whoever got the ball ran like fury before he was murdered)." Most players are Indian—the Iroquois, especially members of the Onondaga tribe, are outstanding. Because Soo-Gui-Ya-Di-Sa-A, the Creator, promised the game would continue even after death, the stick of a deceased Onondaga player is placed in his casket.

*Shinny*

The Wichita claim that the game of shinny—batting a ball or kicking it through goals—was originated by the first man who, traditionally, produced the ball from his left side, the bat from his right. Legend also holds that, after instructing the people how to play shinny, he ordered them to give every newly born boy a ball so that he could learn to move it about. This, in turn, would enable the child to move quickly from place to place when he became a warrior.

Despite this myth, shinny was considered a woman's game by most Indians. However, in some tribes, both sexes played it and contests between men and women were frequently held by the Crows. The game was known to practically every tribe and is often mentioned in tribal lore. The Navajo believed that it was one of the games won by their culture hero, Hatsehogan, during his rivalry with Nohoilpi, god of gambling. Hatsehogan's victory was due to the help given him by a little bird who hid in the ball and carried it toward his opponent's goal. Other tribes also associated shinny with demigods and played ceremonial games in their honor. Shinny contests were often held to celebrate good fortune. At one time, the Makah only played shinny after they had captured a whale.

A shinny field was about three hundred yards long. As in lacrosse, poles usually marked the goals—Menominee women had to hit a pole to score—although certain tribes used blankets strung on a line. There were several variations of the basic game, including one played on ice. Perhaps the most unusual was that of the Indians of California, who lined up in teams and hit the ball in turn. The side that took the least number of strokes to drive the ball through the goal won the game.

54

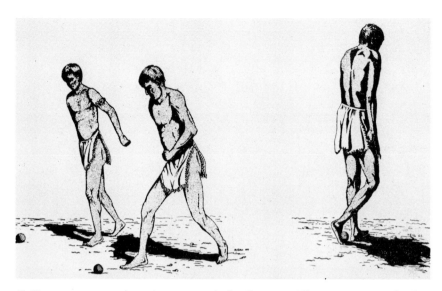

*Ball races were a favorite sport of the Papago. The picture on the left shows the start of a race; the one on the right, the technique of kicking the ball.*

### Ball Race

Kicking sticks, rings of twisted fiber, or wooden or stone balls while racing around a circular course was popular with the Shoshone, California tribes, and the Indians of the Southwest. While no one knows when the ball race originated—the pueblo dwellers claim it was known to the Divine Twins—it must have been early in history. Sticks used for kicking have been found in the cliff dwellings of ancient peoples in Arizona. Then, too, the Navajo, who believe high winds will develop if ball races are held at any season but the spring, hold that their ancestors were taught to run kicking races by a god.

While only two individuals might run a ball race, usually it was a team competition in which the contestants kicked the ball either in turn or whenever they had an opportunity. Intertribal races were common. Among these was the twenty-mile race between the Papago and the Pima. The latter—who excelled at the sport—claimed that they could run faster while kicking a ball because it "carried" them along.

Races were also run between neighboring pueblos. Those taking part were forbidden to bet, but everyone else placed wagers. In order to determine who would win, gamblers placed two balls at one end of a water-filled container. If the ball representing their team was the first to float to the opposite end, they were confident of victory. If they lost, they never blamed the runners but attributed their ill fortune to evil spirits. To avoid the powerful sorcery of these demons, runners consulted shamans and wore charms made of deer hoofs to give them speed. Because a ball that was kicked off the course might wedge between roots or rocks and be very difficult to dislodge, Hopi runners relied on magic to keep their balls flying far and straight. They pasted rabbit fur and hairs taken from fast horses or from the toes of famous runners on them.

While speed was important, it took considerable stamina to run the forty-mile course in six to eight hours, as it was laid out over extremely rough terrain. Along the way, runners were cheered by their friends—who also watched to see that the other team did not touch the ball with their hands—and comforted by their wives. As their husbands passed, the women gave them showers with dipperfuls of water. Meanwhile, the managers of the race kept track of its progress with a circle made up of as many stones as there were laps. As each circuit was completed, a stone was removed.

Ball races played an important role in the religious practices of southwestern tribes. The Keres ran them in the spring, believing that it would call the gods' attention to their need for rain. After the race, they buried the kicking stick used by the winning team in a cornfield. In times of drought, Zuñi men ran short races against women, using a stick decorated with symbolic lightning. But the most sacred ball races of the Zuñi were held at planting time.

In these contests, three to six of the faster runners from each of the four sides of a pueblo competed. Every Zuñi boy hoped to be one of those chosen to run when he reached manhood. Therefore, he began practicing when only a tot by kicking a stick on his way home from the cornfields where youngsters spent the day scaring off crows. But even if a lad did become one of the racers, he might not get the chance to run—if an owl was heard hooting the night before the race, it was called off. On the other hand, a shooting star was considered a good omen.

The "Priests of the Bow" were in charge of Zuñi ceremonial ball races. They not only laid out the course with sacred meal and blessed the runners, setting their hair so it would not fall over their eyes as they ran, but also conducted religious rites before the contest.

*Double Ball*

The Pawnee, along with many other tribes, have a legend telling how a boy and a girl were carried through the sky by a ball. Such tales may have led to the development of double ball. In this game, two balls or billets connected by a thong are cast with a stick. Usually, both balls were the size of an indoor baseball but there was a variation in their shapes. Those of the Fox were oblong and filled with sand, the Hupa's resembled bottles, while the Paiute dispensed with the connecting strap by plaiting a single, long leather cylinder with a narrow middle section.

With the exception of a few tribes, double ball was a woman's game. According to legend, it was given them by Bright-Shining-Woman (the moon), who also taught females how to pack household goods and to care for their families while on the trail.

To score, the ball, which could not be handled, was passed or thrown from one player to another with a slightly curved stick two to six feet long until it reached a goal. Some tribes used crotched sticks for goals and, to count, the ball had to catch on them. The Omaha marked their goals with mounds of dirt and players had to cast the ball over them. There was no regulation playing field—some were over a mile in length.

Despite the fact that double ball was generally considered a woman's game—among the Missisauga it was played mostly by unmarried females—young boys of some tribes engaged in the sport. The Hupa tell of one lad who went to the home of the gods at the western edge of the world and challenged them to play double ball. He won every game and started homeward, expecting a hero's welcome. But on his arrival he discovered that, while he thought he had only been away for a few weeks, it really had been for years and all his friends and family had died.

*Football*

The warning cry "Block that pass!" was never heard when the Indians played football. Throwing the ball with the hands was forbidden. To score, a team had to kick the ball through upright poles or between lines drawn on the snow. Players pushed and shoved one another, but tackling was considered unfair. "They never," wrote one chronicler, "strike up another by the heels as we do, not accepting it praiseworthy to purchase a goal by such an advantage."

It appears that the Indians specialized in defensive rather than offensive plays. William Wood, who watched Massachusetts' tribes, reported that "it might take a side two days to get a goal." While Wood was convinced that one Englishman could "beat ten Indians at football," Roger Williams theorized that the redmen were handicapped "because of their naked feet."

Incidentally, Williams approved of the absence of quarreling when bettors settled their wagers after a game.

Children and adults of both sexes competed in football. The method of play varied from tribe to tribe. In California, the ball was kicked successively by players lined up on the field. On the other hand, the Micmac engaged in scrimmages—after an umpire rolled the ball between the teams, both tried to kick a goal. One California tribe had a unique rule—the men kicked the ball, the women tossed it in baskets. Eskimo women would have scorned this special privilege. They prided themselves on their kicking ability. Indeed, no Indians enjoyed football more than the Eskimos who claimed that the Northern Lights were ghosts playing the game with a walrus skull for a ball.

### Pitch, Toss, and Catch

Besides engaging in complicated ball games, the Indians also enjoyed tossing balls to one another, bouncing them, and throwing them at targets. The Eskimos were adept at whipping a sealskin ball toward a goal by leather thongs attached to a club. Although the goals were only one hundred yards apart, scoring was difficult. A team had to keep the ball in the air because, if it fell to the ground, it was lost to the opposition.

Whipping was but one of many minor ball games enjoyed by the Indians. A common pastime for women was to strike a large ball downward with the hand and kick it upward with the foot. The winner was the individual who did this the most times. A similar game was played by Cheyenne girls. They would kick a ball into the air until either their foot or the ball touched the ground.

Maximilian, Prince of Weld, who visited the Mandan in 1843, told of a game in which a ball decorated with porcupine quills was dropped alternately onto the foot and knee, tossed up, and dropped again. If it was missed, the ball passed to another player.

The Abnaki who played a form of volleyball were very clever at keeping a ball in the air for long periods. Other tribes excelled in juggling. Zuñi mothers made small clay balls for their sons to use for this purpose. Eskimo girls were skilled jugglers, but they were no match for Shoshone women who juggled while running races.

Both the Eskimos and certain Pacific Coast tribes played "catch" with four players forming a square. But instead of throwing the ball to their partner in an opposite corner, they batted it with the open palm. Tlingit children tossed a ball back and forth and lost possession of it if they dropped it. This form of "catch" was played by adults of many tribes. But according to George Cartwright (1792), most Indians were "very bad catchers."

Perhaps the most unusual of all Indian ball games was played in California. Standing in a line, each player tried to cast a ball with his foot farther than any of his competitors. Actually, no one sent the ball a great distance. It was made of stone!

# 5. GAMES OF DEXTERITY—
# FOR TRAINING

*"Skill to do comes of doing."*

The purpose of many of the redman's pastimes was to teach both adults and youngsters the techniques needed to become successful hunters and trained warriors. Boys were encouraged to take part in these activities by their fathers, who believed it was a parent's duty to give sons "a bundle of habits to carry along the Trail of Old Age."

## Archery

Although certain Indians fought with spears or clubs, the redman's most common weapon was the bow and arrow. Similarly, while specially designed spears and clubs were used for hunting, the majority of Indians employed bows and arrows to kill game. Because of their dependence upon archery, the natives of the New World developed a number of games designed to improve their skill with a bow. Thompson River braves engaged in competitions in which they attempted to duplicate Robin Hood's legendary feat of standing a "bow-shot away" from a reed stuck in the ground and splitting it with an arrow.

Bundles of grass served as targets for the Plains Indians while the Omaha set a moccasin on a pole, rode by it at full gallop, and shot from under their mounts' necks. The yucca, a desert plant that provided the Indians of the Southwest with food, drink, and weaving material, furnished the Navajo with marks. They soaked yucca leaves in water, molded them into balls, and used them for targets. Navajo archers also attached yucca balls to blocks of wood with thongs and hung them so that the blocks —which were heavier than the balls—would drop, thus making a moving target.

A number of tribes, particularly in the Southwest, shot at concealed targets. While their playmates stood forty to fifty feet away with their backs turned, Zuñi boys would hide a wad of

*Old prints of an Indian boy and a warrior with bows and arrows*

cornhusks in the ground and make several mounds of dirt to confuse their rivals. The latter then shot at the spot where they thought the wad was hidden. If they missed or their arrows failed to penetrate the wad, they forfeited an arrow to the boy who had hidden it.

The Pottawatomi also hid their targets, made of bark, by covering them with mounds of dirt. Usually, teams consisting of two men on a side competed in shooting at them. Both sides buried bark at either end of an agreed-upon span and a member of each team stood beside it. Taking turns, each contestant shot at the target near his partner. The arrow that came the closest scored one point, a direct hit, five points. Ten points won a game, but if two competitors struck the same target, neither scored.

During the corn harvest festival of the Tewa, groups of boys drew circles of various sizes on the ground in which each one stuck an arrow. Then, standing some distance off, they attempted to shoot the other players' arrows out of the circles. If they succeeded, they kept the arrows.

However, Indian youngsters, like their fathers, preferred shooting at moving objects. A favorite target was a buffalo (bison) hide dragged along the ground. Pima boys not only shot at a very small moving target but also bet one another they could hit it. In this game they formed a circle and the fastest runner in the group moved along the outside edge, dragging a bundle of leaves as a target. A contestant who hit the bundle won all the arrows that the others had wagered, but he had to give a certain percentage of them to the runner. In another game, teams of Pima boys would line up about thirty yards apart and shoot at a prickly-pear cactus. Only the best archers took part in this competition because it was played for high stakes, one bow being considered equal in value to twenty arrows.

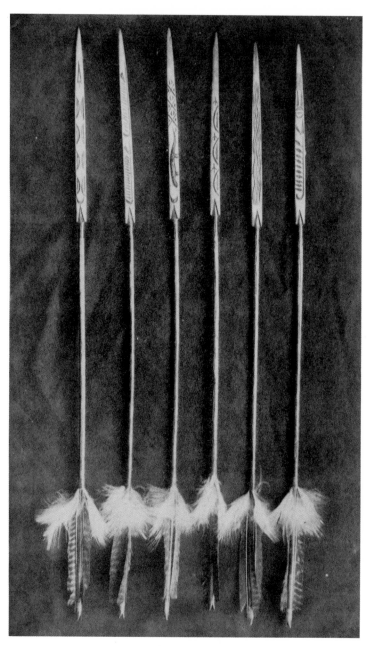

*Kiowa gaming arrows which were thrown by hand. The symbolic designs on the shaft are so old that their meaning has been forgotten for decades.*

But no bets were made by young Sioux when they shot at a piece of cactus fastened to a stick. The plant was held high by a boy who would weave and dodge while the others shot at the cactus. Because the boy who carried the target personified the plant, he supposedly became angry when it was hit and chased the archer whose arrow had found its mark.

The Haida and other tribes of the Northwest Coast played a game which began by all the players shooting arrows into a tree until one became lodged in its branches. Then everyone except the owner of the arrow tried to shoot it free. Each time they failed, they forfeited an arrow to the owner of the target.

While dislodging an arrow from a tree took considerable skill, a bowman had to be exceptionally proficient to win in some other games. Among these were the contests in which an archer attempted to control the flight of his arrow so that, when it fell, its feathers crossed the feathers of another arrow on the ground. Traditionally, this game and its many variations were first played by the Found-in-Grass Twins. Central figures in many Arapaho myths, these legendary brothers correspond to the Divine Twins of southwestern tribes.

Not only did the Indians have to be expert marksmen but also they had to have the ability to shoot a number of arrows in rapid succession. Otherwise a hunter might be mauled by a wounded animal or a warrior be momentarily defenseless on the battlefield. To master the techniques of "rapid-fire" archery, the Indians practiced by playing games.

Young Mandan men engaged in contests in which each archer strove to have more arrows in the air at one time than any of his rivals. Holding a bundle of arrows in the left hand, a competitor shot his first arrow in a high arc, so that it would remain aloft as long as possible, then released the others as fast as he could draw the bow string. The winner won all the arrows shot by the other players.

Southwestern tribesmen prided themselves on their ability to hold a bow in their right hand, toss a bundle of grass wrapped in willow bark into the air with the left hand, and hit it before it fell to the ground. They were also skilled at *tcomalt maitceke* (to shoot the bundle low). In this game, the target was thrown forward rather than upward.

Similar games aimed at teaching archers to draw their bows quickly and shoot accurately were played by many tribes. Usually, the target was a wisp of straw cast into the air by a companion. The Crow version of this sport was more complicated. One man would hold a bundle of grass between his index and second finger as they rested on the arrow. When the arrow was released, the grass flew into the air and his opponent tried to hit it. If he did, he won an arrow.

### Snow Snake

A favorite winter pastime of northern tribes was hurling flat or round rods so that they would slide along crusted snow or smooth ice. The object of this game was to see whose rod—which might be ten feet long—traveled the greatest distance. When cast by an expert, a rod could glide anywhere from six hundred to thirteen hundred feet.

Because one end of the rods—which legend holds stem from the war clubs of the Divine Twins—was often carved to represent the eyes and mouth of a reptile, this game is known as snow snake. However, "snow snake" is a general term used to classify a number of games in which darts, rods, sliders made of animal bones or horn, or spears were either thrown along the ground or cast into the air. All of these activities not only provided recreation but also helped the redman develop the dexterity and strength needed to hurl a javelin at a distant target with accuracy.

Some tribes skimmed their snow snakes over any suitable

*Menominee brave holding snow snake preparatory to throwing. From a painting (about 1895) by Mary Irvin Wright.*

surface. Others cast them along a marked course. The Penobscot made a track in the snow for their rods by dragging a boy down a hill by his legs. Cree snow-snake players erected four barriers along the course they laid out on an ice-covered slope. The rods—which were not thrown but slid downhill by their own weight—had to jump these hazards and still stay on the track. Chippewa boys used the ridges made by the wind on snow banks to guide their short snakes, while their fathers employed a low mound of snow to send their snakes upward before beginning their slide.

All forms of snow snake, including the game of throwing a feathered spear tipped with horn so that it glanced off the ground and continued its flight, were played mainly by men. While competitions between individuals were commonplace, the most exciting contests were between teams which competed in intra-tribal matches. Because of the honors paid to the victors, Indian boys, hoping to become champions, began playing snow snake with short sticks or reeds when very young. Pawnee youngsters threw willow javelins, and the individual who hurled his the farthest won his rivals' spears. When a boy had accumulated enough spears, his grandmother wove his trophies into a mat to celebrate his victories.

While men and boys engaged in snow snake, girls and women tossed darts. Certain tribes threw them at targets. Others vied to throw them the greatest distance. Cree women slid darts down a curving track hollowed out of the snow on a hillside. The Arapaho dart game was enjoyed by both sexes; boys played the girls; men, the women. It consisted of holding a horn-tipped stick horizontally, swinging it back and forth, then suddenly casting it forward with a sweeping motion that caused it to slide along the ground.

Dart-throwing contests and snow-snake matches were exciting events for both competitors and spectators. But there was far more action when the Seneca played *da-ya-no-ta-yen-da-qua* (snow boat). In this game, miniature canoes whittled out of hardwood were raced down snow-covered slopes along trenches into which water had been poured to form ice. A slight keel on the rounded bottoms of the canoes enabled them to remain

*Carl Bodmer drew this picture of a Hidatsa winter village near Fort Clark, North Dakota, in 1833. Two braves play hoop and pole on the snow. Note the earth lodges in background.*

upright during their descent. Except for giving his craft a starting push—which set the rattles hung on it vibrating—a competitor had no control over a canoe. But he could mark its progress by watching the feather fastened to the stern.

### Hoop and Pole

Most tribes north of Mexico played hoop and pole—throwing arrows, darts, or spears at a rolling hoop. Harpooning the target did not count. It had to be hit so that the pole either fell on top of, or underneath, various points of the hoop's interior webbing.

Like certain games of snow snake, hoop and pole provided training in marksmanship. It also developed muscles and tested players' stamina. Meanwhile, no Indian game drew more heavily on the redman's religious beliefs. The Apache claim that one of the Ghons—minor deities who gave man agriculture, crafts, and medicine—taught them the game. According to the Pawnee, they were instructed in the techniques of hoop and pole by Spider Woman, whose magic supposedly controlled the size of buffalo herds. Moreover, Spider Woman promised the Pawnee that as long as they played hoop and pole, hundreds of bison calves would be born every year. The Caddo, who called their poles "bulls" and their hoops "cows," believed that one of their ancestors originated the pastime after seeing bison play it in a dream.

*Apaches engaging in hoop and pole. Photographer and date not recorded, Fort Apache, Arizona.*

Meanwhile, the Navajo maintain that their ancestors played hoop and pole in the lower world. But the Arapaho say the game was invented by an old woman to amuse a boy she found in a stand of high grass. He became an expert with the pole and, as a result, his spear never failed to find its mark.

The nettings of the hoops varied as much as the tales of their origins. Certain tribes merely divided their hoops into sections. Others filled them with intricate patterns. In the Southwest, each quarter of a hoop was colored symbolically to represent the points of the compass, the homes of the four winds, and the circle of day and night. Other hoops were made up of concentric circles of netting, were decorated with beads or feathers, or contained radial spokes. Each of these divisions or decorations had varying values.

Irrespective of their tribes, all Indians believed that the netted hoop had a divine origin. Some traced it back to the webbed shields of the war gods. Others said it stemmed from the sacred web woven by Spider Woman and was a symbol of her protection. This is the reason Chippewa parents placed small netted shields on their babies' cradles, the Navajo wore circlets of woven grass, and many Indians placed tiny netted shields in their hair as a combination ornament and good-luck charm. Incidentally, netted shields also were important accessories in the Sun and Ghost Dances. Today, netted shields hang from many Hopi kachina masks.

Although Jicarilla Apache tradition states that hoop and pole was invented by the White Bead Woman for her sons, the children of the sun and moon, Apache women were not allowed to play the game or to watch it. Klamath women had more freedom. They participated in a version of hoop and pole in which facing contestants tried to pierce a hoop with an awl. But Cheyenne women were barred from the game. When this tribe played, an umpire rolled the hoop away from the two contestants. They ran after it and tried to throw their poles into the sections of the netting that had the highest value.

There were many other variations of the basic game. The Iroquois stood in line and hurled their poles at the hoop as it passed. Other tribes did not cast their poles until the hoop began to wobble just before it toppled to the ground. Still others threw their poles ahead of the hoop, causing it to fall across them. In the Blackfoot variant, the players shot an arrow at the hoop just as it passed a specified place. One of the most unusual hoop-and-pole games was that of the Eskimos. They hung up a small, flat piece of ivory in which a hole had been bored and attempted to poke a stick through the opening.

Although most tribes played hoop and pole on any available flat surface, the Mandan laid out smooth passageways for their hoops. The Creeks who played chunky—a form of hoop and pole in which a stone ring was used rather than the traditional netted hoop—built large enclosed courts. These "stadiums" had sloping sides so that spectators could sit on them and watch chunky competitions.

Chunky was very popular with southeastern tribes who engaged in it from morn to night. James Adair, who watched them in 1775, could not understand the players' enthusiasm. He called chunky "running hard labor." Adair reported that the stone rings used by the Choctaw were kept "with the strictest religious care from one generation to another, and are exempted from being buried with the dead."

While there is no record of women participating in the basic hoop-and-pole game, there was no restriction on their shooting arrows or throwing darts at netted rings. However, when Hopi women shot arrows into cornhusk wads, it was not for recreation. They were symbolizing lightning striking a cornfield.

While women of certain tribes threw darts or shot arrows at netted wheels during religious rites, men usually played cere-

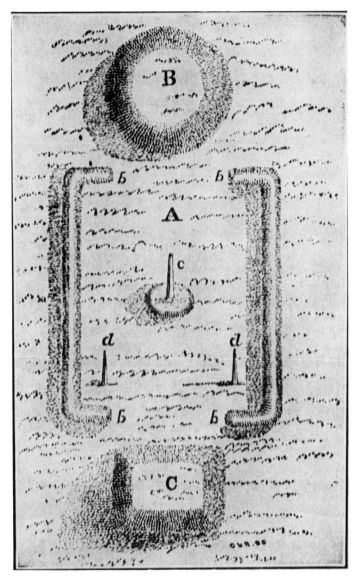

*Drawing of a chunk yard in Georgia by William Bartram, one of the first American ornithologists, who lived with the Indians in the late eighteenth century. The yard is surrounded by banks where the spectators sat. "A" marks the playing field and "c" the chunk pole. The tribal round house was located at "B" and "C" was the public square. The two poles marked "d" were used to torture captives.*

*Throwing darts at netted rings was a popular pastime of Indian women who, in most tribes, were forbidden to play hoop and pole.*

monial hoop-and-pole games. These ritual contests were very sacred to the Zuñi, and the priests closely supervised the matches held in honor of the war gods or to ask deities for rain. Other tribes believed that an individual who competed in a formal hoop-and-pole contest and won would gain great wealth. Thus, before engaging in such a game, the Apaches offered special prayers and chants.

Hoop and pole was also played to cure sickness and to foretell the future. The Sauk and Fox tribes were convinced that if they shot an arrow into a certain section of the netting of a buried hoop, Apenaweni, the spirit of sickness, would vanish. Meanwhile, Kiowa braves paid for the right to throw darts at their shaman's hoop, believing that their success or failure indicated how they would fare in the days ahead.

Because of the supposedly magic power of the hoop, it is not surprising that the redman's mythology is crammed with tales of hoops that kept on rolling and turned into mountains or other natural objects. Other stories tell of players who cast their hoops in a forbidden direction, and, for punishment, had to perform difficult deeds. There are also eerie accounts of hoop-and-pole contests between a sorcerer and a demigod. The latter always wins, throws the evil magician into a fire, and brings his victims back to life.

### Ring and Pin

Many Indian games had no counterparts in the Old World. However, ring and pin is quite similar to the ancient European pastime of cup and ball. The latter is played with a ball attached to a stick which has a cup fixed on one end. The pur-

*Skull used in* ajegaung, *the Eskimo version of ring and pin.*

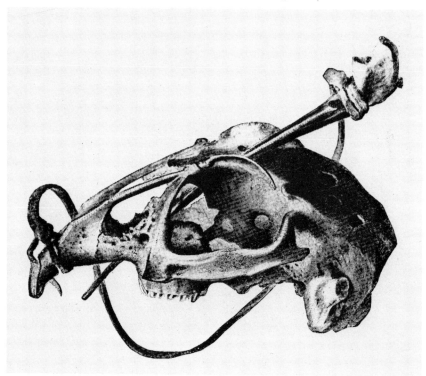

pose of the game is to throw the ball upward and catch it in the cup as many times as possible. In ring and pin, the Indians tied thorns, sharp slivers of bone, or wooden needles to perforated targets with a thong, held the pin horizontally, the target hanging loosely, then cast it upward and forward. As the target passed the pin, they stabbed at it.

It took a keen eye, supple wrist, and fast reactions to pierce the rings, which varied in form and material. Algonquian tribes used a string of bones which nestled inside one another; southwestern Indians employed pumpkin rinds or a series of rings fashioned from gourds; while the Paiute preferred rodent skulls. Baffin Land Eskimos made their targets from hares' skulls; the Klamath utilized bundles of pine twigs. Other tribes used bullrushes, wads of moose hair, pieces of buckskin, loops of beads, or musk-ox horns.

The Passamaquoddy made their rings from a tree-growing fungus which they called *squaw-oc-l'moss-wal-dee* (the swamp

*A ring and pin set from the Southwest. The rings are fashioned from dried gourds.*

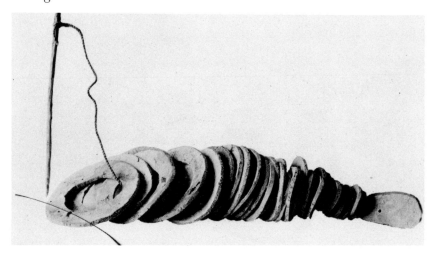

woman's dishes). Strangely enough, the Passamaquoddy feared the evil magic of the legendary swamp woman. Therefore, their children never played with toadstools, believing that, if they did, she would punish them.

Not only did targets vary among the tribes but so did scoring. In some variants of the game, the ring—which was symbolic of the war god's shield—could only be pierced through one opening. In others, the ring was punctured with numerous holes of various values. Then, too, certain tribes did not connect ring to pin. For example, Huron children tossed corn-leaf balls into the air and tried to catch them on a pointed stick.

Ring and pin was generally played indoors during the winter. The Klamath, who competed in *shapashspatcha* (to split the moon) with a bullrush-pith ball hung from a braided strap, believed that the more they played, the sooner spring would come. Usually, only two people took part in a game of ring and pin. However, team contests were held by some tribes.

While ring and pin was a favorite of gamblers, it was considered a lovers' game by the Cheyenne, Passamaquoddy, and Hupa. When a Hupa youth fell in love, he announced his desire to marry the maiden of his choice by inviting her to play. Before a Passamaquoddy brave called on his loved one, he fashioned a ring and pin from an eight-inch pointed bone connected to a cone of moose hair by a fourteen-inch thong. When he arrived at the maiden's dwelling, she brought out skins and the two sat cross-legged on them as they played. He had the first turn and continued throwing the ring until he missed it. When the girl began to play, her caller watched anxiously—if she pierced the target and continued the game he knew his suit was successful. But if she handed him the ring and pin, he knew that she loved another.

Although a jilted brave's pride suffered, he did not experience the pain felt by Indian boys of some tribes when they lost a game of ring and pin. In these contests, the winner had the right to thump his opponent's forehead, pull his hair, or rap him across the knuckles.

## Horse Racing

To the Plains Indian, no possession was more valuable than a fleet horse. Such a mount enabled him to chase bison, raid settlements and wagon trains, swoop down on the horse herds of other tribes, and gallop into battle. These activities not only required a swift horse but also expert horsemanship. The "horse Indians" learned to control their mounts by engaging in sham battles and by racing.

Since practically every young man had acquired a fast horse he had either "stolen, bartered, bought, or captured," there were constant arguments in every camp as to which brave owned the fastest pony. The races that settled these disputes were usually accompanied by gambling on the outcome by both spectators and participants alike.

Before a race, a Nez Percé warrior painted red and yellow stripes on his face and on the body of his horse. Because smearing enough paint to cover the animal's true color took considerable time, the Nez Percé preferred either piebald or gray horses. Both are not only easier to color but also blend into the landscape when tethered on the prairie. After painting his mount, the brave colored its mane and tail, usually making one black, the other red. In addition to painting the tail, the warrior also twined it with leather strips interlaced with feathers. Sometimes so many feathers were used that, from a distance, a horse appeared to have two tails.

But not all Indian horse races required such elaborate preparations. Nor did the contestants always bet. Prince Maximilian of Weld reported that the Indians living near Fort Pierre, South Dakota, were so dependent upon white traders that they no longer hunted and, as a result, were "consequently poor." But, His Highness added, they passed the time racing their horses.

Just as modern teen-agers foolishly try to impress girls by driving their automobiles recklessly, Indian youths, hoping to attract the attention of the maidens in their villages, would race their horses. There is a description of one of these contests in *The Oregon Trail* by Francis Parkman. In telling of the breaking-up of an encampment of Oglala Sioux he wrote: "Young braves gaudy with paint and feathers, rode in groups among the crowd, often galloping, two or three at once, along the line to try the speed of their horses."

# 6. CHILDREN'S GAMES

*"He'll play a small game..."*

With the exception of certain ritual competitions, Indian youngsters played most of the games enjoyed by their parents. In addition, they amused themselves by running races, jumping, wrestling, and walking on their knees. Eskimo children delighted in paddling kayaks or being thrown repeatedly into the air while sitting on a walrus hide. Young Sioux relished sliding on sleds made of a bison's rib bones. Many of the games played by Indian boys and girls were identical with those engaged in by children throughout the world—blindman's buff, follow the leader, hide and seek, ring-around-a-rosy, and tug of war.

Nevertheless, certain toys common to the Old World were practically unknown to Indian youngsters. For example, although Zuñi boys used their planting sticks as stilts and an early chronicler of Mayan customs described a dancer on stilts honoring Yaccocahmut, the bird god, few Indian children ever saw a pair of stilts. Similarly, while Pawnee lore tells of a maiden who had the power to attract buffalo while in a swing, most Indian youngsters never experienced the fun of swinging. However, Teton children did hang swings—with blankets for seats—from leaning trees every autumn.

*"The youth at their exercises." From an engraving by De Bry after a
drawing by Le Moyne, who visited the Timucua Indians of Florida in
1564–65.*

Generally speaking, boys and girls did not play together, although both sexes often engaged in the same games. Boys usually followed one set of rules and girls another. Girls, like adult
women, were forbidden to participate in certain games while
others were only played by boys because they were exceptionally rough.

### Boys' Games

Indian boys learned to be bold warriors through play.
Therefore, a number of their favorite games were actually dangerous. The players threw clods of dirt, firebrands, or hot mud
at one another, chewed leaves and spat them in an opponent's
eye, or engaged in sham fights in which reeds were used as
spears. Because a wounded warrior was expected to ignore
pain, "captives" taken in mock battles were tested by having

81

their heads pounded, fingers pulled, and feet twisted.

Other games taught the techniques of stalking animals, flushing birds, or finding eggs. One pastime of Eskimo boys was mimicking seal hunters. Every player had a miniature harpoon made by his father, a perforated piece of seal skin prepared by his mother, and the hip bone of a seal. Taking turns, each player, making a noise like a seal blowing, moved his skin-covered bone back and forth while the others tried to harpoon it. Any player who did so, won both the skin and bone.

In some games the participants pretended they were medicine men. Actually, "making believe" played an important role in the games of Indian children. In the Sioux pastime of *ichap-sil echunpi* (making the wood jump), a group of boys would mark off an imaginary river that was frozen solid and throw rocks at a billet in the middle of the "ice."

Most Indian boys could join a game of stick ball on the street in any modern city without difficulty. Various forms of "tip cat" were played by many tribes throughout the year. But Cheyenne youngsters would be shocked to see anyone today spinning a top during the summer. They stopped playing with tops in the spring, convinced that if they continued to use them, hair would cover their bodies.

Not only was top-spinning a widespread pastime among the Indians but also it was a very ancient one. Tops—and popguns—have been excavated from the sites of prehistoric villages in Peru. While the majority of Indian tops were whipped with a cord to make them spin, some had wooden or bone spindles which, when twisted, set the tops in motion. Other tops were kept turning by being lashed with buckskin quirts.

Indian boys fashioned tops from bone, clay, horn, ivory, or wood. Pueblo dwellers whittled out tops and cut holes in their sides to make them hum. However, some authorities state that they were taught to do this by Europeans. The most unusual top was made by the practical jokers among the Eskimo living on the shores of Hudson's Bay. They would coax one of their number to sit on a large top, then spin it with sticks until the victim became seasick.

Most Indians spun their tops on ice. While the Niska competed to see who could keep their tops rotating the longest, the Oglala Sioux attempted to keep their tops within a square. Other Sioux marked off a rectangle on the ice and sought to knock their opponents' tops out of it with their tops. Thompson River boys—and their fathers—cast bone-pinned tops onto those of their rivals in order to split them. Eskimo boys combined top-spinning with racing. They would start their tops in front of an igloo, then run around the dwelling, trying to get back to their starting point before the tops stopped spinning.

Like all boys, Indian lads enjoyed making a noise. Sioux youngsters made "bull-roarers" out of a piece of straight, flat wood connected to a handle by a strip of hide. Grasping the handle, they whirled the stick in a circle above their heads and simulated the sound of wind blowing. As a matter of fact, some tribes believed that bull-roarers caused high winds. Therefore, Apache boys were forbidden to make them, while Hopi youngsters were allowed to play with them only in the spring when there was no danger of crops being flattened by a gale. Paiute parents banned the use of bull-roarers at any time. Members of this tribe would not even swish a switch in fear their action might summon one of the wind spirits.

Another whirling toy, which was known to the ancient cliff dwellers of Arizona, consisted of a flat piece of bone, a section of a gourd, shell, or hide, or a pottery disc threaded with cords. By alternately pulling or relaxing the cords, the suspended article spun vigorously, making a loud buzz.

*Havasupai girls at play. They seem more interested in the camera than their game.*

## Girls' Games

Although Indian girls began helping with household chores at the age of eight, they still found time for play. They enjoyed racing, swimming, tag, throwing snowballs, and coasting as much as their brothers did. But girls rarely slid on sleds made of willow boughs or animal bones. They coasted on hides, in the process softening them and removing the hair.

The favorite pastime of younger girls was "playing house." They would act out all the duties performed by their mothers and pretend dolls were babies. In most tribes, the mothers fashioned their daughters' dolls from bark, buckskin, clay, cornhusks, plant fibers, or wood, but among the Carib, dollmaking was the father's task.

84

Many Indian dolls were crude, others were lifelike. Those of Eskimo girls had pegs that enabled the arms, legs, and heads to be moved. Buckskin dolls were often beaded, but the most colorful Indian dolls are the vividly painted ones passed out by kachina dancers during the rituals of the pueblo dwellers. Technically, these are not playthings, as they have a religious significance.

Dolls were "fed" from miniature dishes and pots whittled out of wood, cut from birch bark, or molded from clay. In nearly every tribe, parents fashioned a "Noah's Ark" for their children, carving the animals from wood or stuffing fur with grass. Eskimo youngsters not only played with excellent bone replicas of animals, birds, and boats, but also with a mechanical toy carved from ivory. It consisted of a bird which bobbed its head as if pecking when strings were pulled.

Indian girls, however, did not always play quietly with dolls and other toys. They made as much noise as their brothers did when blowing whistles. Incidentally, whistles used either in religious ceremonies or as playthings were manufactured by the redman centuries ago. Thousands of bone or pottery whistles have been found in the sites of prehistoric settlements.

Although the noise made by a group of whistle-blowing girls was deafening, it was no louder than the shrieks of laughter and cries of warning that accompanied games of tag. There were dozens of variations of tag. Nootka girls combined "snap the whip" and tag in their favorite game. They would run sidewise, holding hands, and suddenly let go. Any girl who lost her balance had to chase the others. Any individual she caught was "out." Blackfoot maidens formed a line and their leader would execute twists and turns in her attempt to tag the girl at the end of the line. If she succeeded, she dropped back a place and the tagged girl became "it." Hopi girls laid out a complicated maze and, if one of their number left the path, she was barred from the game. Moreover, all the other players tagged her by giving her a tap on the head.

Like their parents, girls of northwestern tribes held laughing competitions. In these contests, the players did everything they could to make their rivals laugh. Klamath maids vied with one another to see which one of them could hold her breath the longest. But this too was a noisy pastime—after inhaling deeply the players would run while yelling at the top of their voices until out of breath. The girl who ran the greatest distance was the winner. Nookta girls played a similar game with fern fronds. The girl who broke off the most leaves while holding her breath was declared the winner.

Evidently, Chippewa parents sometimes tired of the noise made by playing children. At any rate, adults of this tribe frequently organized "the game of silence." All the members of the family would sit in the center of their wigwam and the grown-ups would sing humorous songs about animals. Then everyone sat silently, and the child who was the last to speak won a prize.

### Cat's-cradle

Making figures with string, leather thongs, or animal sinews looped around the fingers is a pastime of primitive peoples throughout the world. While all of these groups create their own characteristic designs, many of the figures are universally constructed.

In playing cat's-cradle—so-called because of the appearance of the basic design—the hands are held with the palms facing and the fingers upward. After making a relatively large loop, the player weaves a varying number of smaller loops which he moves from the fingers of one hand to those of the other in a definite sequence. When complicated figures are formed, addi-

86

*Making string figures is a popular pastime of primitive peoples through-out the world. This cat's-cradle is held by its weaver, a Navajo.*

tional loops are made with the aid of the teeth, toes, or a stick stuck in the ground. Frequently, two players join in creating an intricate design, passing the "cradle" back and forth.

It is believed that cat's-cradle originated in ancient China. The game was probably brought to the New World by migrating huntsmen (the ancestors of the Eskimo) who crossed the land bridge that once connected Asia and North America. But the Navajo claim that the game was taught them by the Spider People. Nevertheless, Navajo tradition maintains that cat's-cradle should only be played in the winter when spiders are asleep.

While the Eskimos did not share the Navajo conviction that a horrible death would befall any individual a spider saw playing cat's-cradle, they did consider the game a seasonal one. The only time the Eskimos engaged in cat's-cradle was the autumn —hoping that they could keep the sun from falling below the horizon. Nootka children were forbidden cat's-cradle while their fathers were hunting seals. This taboo was based on the belief that if they disobeyed, their fathers would get their fingers caught in the harpoon ropes.

Not only young people enjoyed cat's-cradle. Fierce Apache warriors prided themselves on their ability to create complicated string figures that vanished with a twist of the wrist. Besides forming animals, birds, butterflies, fish, and household utensils, skilled weavers fashioned representations of humans engaged in various activities. In some tribes, experts at cat's-cradle also performed tricks with string. A favorite stunt of the Makah was to tie a cord around their necks, allow onlookers to see if the knot was tight, then jerk one end of the cord. As they did, the cord fell to the ground—it was tied with a false knot. A similar deception was practiced by Maya magicians. They placed a rope that *appeared* to be cut into two sections in their mouths, made a series of facial contortions, and spat the rope onto the ground. When the spectators picked the rope up, it was in one piece.

Listing all the games the Indians played would fill several books the size of this one. Along with the pastimes described on these pages, the redman enjoyed dozens of others, ranging from forms of shuttlecock to holding canoe races upstream against the current. Then, too, after the coming of the white man, the Indians borrowed many of his games and created their own versions of cards, checkers, and chess.

However, mention must be made of one of the most unusual games ever played by Indians. It took place in 1906 when the residents of the Hopi town of Oraibi—perhaps the oldest con-

*Front and rear views of battledores used by Indians of the Pacific North-west.*

tinuously inhabited settlement in North America—split into two groups. One of them was made up of conservatives who opposed the "new ways" advocated by the liberals in the tribe. The constant conflict between the two groups created a very unpleasant situation and it seemed impossible to resolve it. Finally, it was suggested that the argument be settled by a tug-of-war.

All agreed—and the conservatives lost. But they did not dis-

*Tewa kiva altar showing gaming reeds.*

play the traditional good sportsmanship of the redman when defeated in a game. All of the conservative group moved out of Oraibi and established a new village.

Today, far more Indians listen to radio and television broadcasts of sporting events than to tribal taletellers recounting the exploits of a mythical player of games. Only in a few tribes—particularly those native to the Southwest—is the rich and ancient game heritage of the redman remembered and old traditions and customs maintained.

But if the prayers and chants sung before an intertribal contest have been forgotten and ritual games are rarely played, the Divine Twins have no reason to complain. The legendary patrons of games must know that modern Indians are as actively engaged in baseball, basketball, football, golf, hockey, and tennis as their ancestors were with hoop and pole, snow snake, and lacrosse.

# INDEX

SIGMUND A. LAVINE was highly active while in college; he wrote features for the *Boston Sunday Post* and covered Boston University sports for two wire services. After receiving his M.A., he taught in a United States Government Indian School at Belcourt, North Dakota, for two years, learned to speak both the Sioux and Cree languages and talk in sign language. He was invited to tribal dances, ceremonies, and Indian Court in reservations throughout Canada and the Northwest.

Sigmund Lavine has taught in the Boston schools for over thirty years and is now an assistant principal. He also lectures and writes literary criticism.

With his wife—and a whippet answering to the unlikely name of Morrisey, the latest in a long line of prize-winning dogs owned by the Lavines—he lives in a house filled with books, fish tanks, historical china, art glass, and the largest privately owned collection of Gilbert and Sullivan material in America. For relaxation the Lavines attend country auctions, go "antiquing," or browse in bookstores, but their greatest pleasure is truck gardening on a piece of rocky New Hampshire land.